TEARS TO INK

Fred G. Di Marco

Father of Nicholas Jordan Di Marco

Fulton Books, Inc.
Meadville, PA

Published by Fulton Books 2021

ISBN 978-1-64952-557-4 (paperback)
ISBN 978-1-63710-399-9 (hardcover)
ISBN 978-1-64952-558-1 (digital)

Printed in the United States of America

ACKNOWLEDGMENTS

All people mentioned below have played a vital role in the events of my life in recent years, whether you knew this or not.

Although this has been the most painful and difficult time I could ever have imagined enduring, all mentioned and more have been paramount in my healing process.

- Nicole Walmsley Brantner, opioid mentor, dear friend, and someone I refer to as my adopted daughter. Nicole's constant love and never-ending support have been instrumental to my healing. To you, Nicole, I will always be grateful.
- Donna Doles, a friend I made due to the opioid crisis, who has spent hours as the editor and reviewer of my poems for *Tears to Ink*.
- Donna Lingo, *Tears to Ink* logo designer, thank you for sharing your talent to create the cover for this book.
- Fil Warner, my best friend, who has been there for me during the loss of my son Nick. I will always be grateful for you love and support.
- Bernard Primiano, best friend, another member of my emotional support system, and provider of the original artwork of *Slay the Dragon*. Many thanks for all your talent and all you do.
- Keith Martin, DEA Cleveland, Ohio. Many thanks to you and your agents for all you do in fighting this opioid crisis.
- Rob Brandt, Robbie's Voice. Thank you for this organization which is bringing awareness and helping so many.
- Chief of Police Matt Vanyo, Olmsted, Ohio. Many thanks for the kindness shown by you and your department during my darkest times.
- Brenda Stewart, The Addicts Parents (TAP). Thank you to this wonderful group of people trying to bring about awareness and change in this battle we fight.

- Ohio CAN (Change Addiction Now) and all the wonderful people involved. Thank you for the support, friendship, and awareness you have provided myself and others.
- PAARI (Police Assisted Addiction & Recovery Initiative). I'm grateful to all of you for the countless hours you are spending to save lives and bring about the needed change. The influence of these departments has done a great deal to help end the stigma and save lives.
- Gloucester Police Chief Leonard Campanello. Thank you for the great work you are doing and for caring enough to help bring about needed change.
- AJ Assad, Abe Haq, and Jose Huerta. My son Nick's friends who cared enough and reached out to me when they knew Nick was out using. They were loyal friends who hoped in doing so that Nick may get help and survive. I will always appreciate their concern. Thanks, guys, he loved you as you love him.
- Tamara M. Larkin, community outreach specialist (FBI-Cleveland Division). Thank you for your compassion and caring.
- Pam Murphy, New Directions counselor. Thank you for all your efforts.
- Greg McNeil, Cover 2 Cover Podcasts. Thank you for providing exposure and awareness.
- And additionally, many thanks to: Andrea Mac Leod Mihelich; TAP; Tracy Carlos, WEWS new anchor; Joseph M. Pinjuh, USAOHN; Michael Tobin, USAOHN; Mike DeWine, Ohio governor; Travis and Shelly Bornstein; Breaking Barriers; Samantha Burkhart; Dani Carlson, Channel 19 NEWS; CR Carter; Roseann DeBlasio; Cindy Ferguson DeMaio; Jim Fennel; Barbara Folds; Sgt. Patrick Greenhill; Berea PD; BA Force; Rene Elefleriou; Detective Jay Hadam, Cuyahoga County Sheriff's Department; Higgy Robin Higginbotham; Jerome Sessini, photojournalist for Magnum; Nick Bianco; Heather Bauer; Dr. Nicole Labor, Addiction Assasin; Rachel's Angels; Jim and Laura Cash; Mim Cherrie; Rose DeRoia; Cindy King-Anderson; Sean's to Bridge; Sam Quinones; Dreamland; Anna Ricciadella Zsinko; Susan Rocca; Dr. Stephen R. Sroka; Scott Vanderkarr.

CONTENTS

Nick's high school picture

GOOD NIGHT

Woke up in a fright
From my son screaming at night,

"Oh my God, Nick," was what he said
Hearing that I sprang from my bed.

His twin lay sprawled on the bathroom floor lying at death's closing door.

A needle & spoon lay on the sink,
Of course the worst was all I could think.

"Call 911," was what I said,
As I sat and cradled my son's head.

I tried what I could,
But I felt like my body and mind were made out of wood.

EMS arrived at the scene,
While I prayed, that this was a horrible dream.

They rushed my son to the hospital, while doing everything Humanly possible.

My son's life was stopped meeting this tragic end,
Thanks to a dealer who sold him HEROIN.

Father of Nicholas Jordan Di Marco

DEADLY PROMISES

Sweet promises I carefully whisper in your ear,
To numb the pain and remove that which you fear.

Sad for you it works for such a short time,
The more you use, the more you become mine.

You want nothing more than to stop and be free of me,
Reenter the land of the living trying to embrace your recovery.

If only you could shatter those opioid chains,
Which this addiction has shackled to your brain.

You wanted to escape this world of pain and sorrow,
Hoping you will you live to see tomorrow.

An illusion of the blackest of magic it is to get high,
The plain truth is, it's all just a lie.

A battle rages within your very soul,
As you only wish to be made whole.

But as dark and alone you may think yourself to be,
Many are here to shine the light of recovery.

Take a good look in the mirror and at your face,
It is you we wish to save, as you belong to the human race.

Father of Nicholas Jordan Di Marco

IN MEMORY OF THE LIFE AND DEATH OF NICHOLAS JORDAN DI MARCO

(March 22, 1996–March 9, 2015)

Born on March 22, 1996 in North Olmsted, Ohio along with his twin brother, Adam Joseph. Nick brought forth into this world a bright ray of sunshine. Behind his bright blue eyes were hidden anxiety and depression. There were subtle signs but not readable by the average parent. Nick was highly intelligent (honor roll), school was no challenge, and he became bored quite quickly. While very athletic, Nick hated structure or organized sports. Nick enjoyed doing street tricks on his BMX bike and/or hacky sack. His goal was to become a personal fitness trainer. Quick witted with an infectious laugh, he would create attention ether positive or negative due to his insecurities. He was loved by all that came into contact with him; our lives were made better by being blessed to know him.

By the father of Nicholas Jordan Di Marco

The opioid epidemic has been called the worst drug crisis in American history. Death rates now rival those of AIDS from the 1990s. And with overdoses from heroin and other opioids now killing more than 72,000 people a year, the crisis has led to urgent calls for action.

The epidemic didn't happen overnight. Over the course of more than a decade, it has grown into a problem destroying lives across the nation, regardless of age, race, wealth, or location. Here's a look at how it happened and who is most affected.

Drugs Now Kill More Americans Than Cars

In 1999, there were more than twice as many motor vehicle deaths as fatal drug overdoses. By 2014, those numbers had flipped, with almost 40 percent more deaths from overdoses than car crashes. In all, 29,230 people died in car accidents in 2014, while 47,055 died from drug overdose. Opioid prescriptions tripled over a twenty-year span. These are factual statistics.

WHO KILLED THE ADDICT?

The first that comes to mind of course is the dealer, they're the ones that mixed the fentanyl with that shit.

Then again no one put a gun to their head, it was their Choice so now they woke up dead.

How about the other kids at school?
They didn't like you, you didn't fit in, and you just weren't cool.

Big bad Dad who didn't quite understand said, "Stop right now, be a man."

Mom just wanted you to be happy,
She couldn't or wouldn't see the misery.

The men in blue are so tired of booking you,
You should rot in jail, as they didn't have a clue.

You see first responders when you awoke,
What you hear from them, was they got here too early what a mistake.

It's easy to point a finger and place blame,
I would rather fix it than have the pain.

Father of Nicholas Jordan Di Marco

A PATH OF PAIN

Dedicated to the wonderful group Ohio CAN!

A name is called from a voice filled with sorrow,
After that a pair of shoes are laid down to follow.

Sneakers and stilettos sit side by side,
While the names echo in silence, all the broken hearts you cannot hide.

Once a year they come together to celebrate the love of those that have gone.
Taken by the disease of addiction, so many innocents, this is so wrong!

Something so simple as a pair of shoes,
Creates too long a line of tragic news.

We speak their names and honor their memory,
While working toward saving the others trying to get them into successful recovery.

Forever remembered in our brain and always loved in our heart,
We use that to help the others to get a brand-new start.

Father of Nicholas Jordan Di Marco

facts...
How Is Substance Abuse Childish Behavior?

Drug Rehab Addiction, Addictive Behaviors, Risky Behavior

It might seem like an odd way to think about substance abuse and addiction, but the behaviors are childish and immature. no one can claim ignorance of the negative consequences of drug or alcohol abuse, yet people do it anyway. being impulsive and lacking self-discipline are traits that are common in children and which we are expected to outgrow. so why do drug abusers act like children, and how can they learn to grow up?

Impulsivity, Self-Control, and Drug Abuse

Addict behaviors are like children's—drug abuse, us controlling impulses is something we all have to learn as human beings. We are not born with self-discipline. As young children, we reach for what we want. As we grow older, we learn to control our impulses. Those who fail to learn the skill, for whatever reason, are not as successful. For instance, a study found that teenagers that exhibited strong self-control were more likely to be positive, achieve goals, be self-motivated, and more successful in academics than their impulsive peers.

Research has also found that being impulsive and lacking self-control are traits that may be inherent in some people. We also know that having these traits makes some people more susceptible to drug abuse and addiction. If you can't control your impulses, and if you lack the self-control to turn down a pleasurable drug because of negative consequences, you are more likely to fall into addiction.

A DAD'S DILEMMA

I'm the Dad that much is true,
Then why didn't I know the right things to do?

The disease of addiction held you close in its arms, and I thought I
could keep you away from its charms.

Lack of knowledge, pride and/or shame,
Didn't help to beat this deadly game.

It was my job to keep you safe from harm,
I learned too much after the horses left the barn.

So now that you're gone, what do I do?
The things I did, from my heart were true.

The memory of your face along with speaking your name, are one of
the ways that help me stay sane.

Father of Nicholas Jordan Di Marco

A MOTHER'S WOE

The door opens and you walk in,
Oh my god, where have you been!

A sigh of relief knowing that you are well,
Do you have any idea that you put me through hell?

Mom, you don't understand, it's not really that bad,
If that's so true, then why are you always acting so sad?

You need to stop that much is true,
Don't you see what the drugs are doing to you?

Leave me alone, it's not your problem,
Yes, it is, and what you're doing won't solve them.

I want to help in any way I can,
It just seems that you don't give a damn.

My love for you is unconditional and true,
I just hope it's enough to get you through.

Father of Nicholas Jordan Di Marco

9 Tips For Dealing with and Supporting the Heroin Addict in Your Household without Enabling

1. Learn all you can
2. Pay attention to their "cycle"
3. Get support for yourself from others who understand
4. Understand that addiction is a disease
5. Accept that others will lack empathy for addiction in general
6. Understand that addiction is a "family disease"
7. Do not blame yourself
8. The "E" word (Enabling)
9. Never lose hope

THE OPIOID GAME OF THRONES

Who shall reign upon the opioid throne?
Many wish to rule this all alone.

Doctors for years held the lead with the strength of their pen,
Writing many bogus prescriptions again and again.

Big Pharma had the backing of their R&D, creating an addictive drug
that was just too strong.
Rolling out their armies of beautiful sales reps, while they knew it was
wrong.

The drug cartels would not be left behind,
Driven by greed and power, this was their edge they were looking to
find.

The backstreet chemists in China observed the shift to fentanyl and
its need,
Churning out the bootleg death just to satisfy their greed.

This insidious seat shall not be so easily won,
The masses are gathering to have this reign undone.

With shields of Prevention we will protect our family.
A sword of enforcement to keep the enemy away from you and me.

Donning the armor of Treatment to protect us from their lies.
With a helmet of Education to help us get wise.

Boots of Recovery to aid us along our long trail,
With love and support so they do not fail.

Father of Nicholas Jordan Di Marco

TWO

Two years ago, today the world became a darker place.
All I have left is memories and pictures of your face.

They say time flies, but grief and loss keep you grounded, while the
unanswered questions in your head make you feel confounded.

We look back and think of what was and then what should be,
And are just left in misery.

Anger, guilt, love, and pain,
Just looking for someone to explain.

Choice or fate who's to say,
I just wish you were here another day.

Father of Nicholas Jordan Di Marco

THE RECOVERY FLOWER

A flower that used to be so extremely rare,
Now it's beginning to be seen here and there.

To successfully grow this beautiful plant,
You first must overcome the idea that you can't.

It will take time and the utmost patience to nurture this seed,
Love and support it most surely needs.

With the light of education like it was heaven sent,
And its roots firmly planted in a soil of solid treatment.

Let's not forget the rain of self-worth,
When it blooms, what an amazing rebirth!

Of the most beautiful sight this is to see,
The blossoming flower of Recovery!

Father of Nicholas Jordan Di Marco

1980 NEJM LETTER—THE GENESIS OF THE OPIOID CRISIS?

Deborah Brauser
June 06, 2017

The now infamous "Porter and Jick" letter published in the New England Journal of Medicine (NEJM) in 1980, which has been cited more than 600 times over the years, may have been the spark that ignited North America's opioid crisis, new research suggests.

The original, one-paragraph letter was written by principal investigator Herschel Jick, MD, Boston University Medical Center, Waltham, Massachusetts, and his assistant and lead author, Jane Porter.

In just five sentences, the duo reported that among 39,946 hospitalized medical patients, of whom 11,882 received at least one narcotic, there were only four documented cases of addiction—and only one of these cases was considered major.

The letter ended by stating, "the development of addiction is rare in medical patients with no history of addiction."

A new Correspondence piece published in the June 1 issue of the NEJM reports that although the letter was not heavily referenced, it has been cited more than 600 times, with many authors "grossly misrepresenting" the conclusion.

"It's hard to overstate how important this letter was to the ensuing opioid crisis," corresponding author David N. Juurlink, MD, PhD, Sunnybrook Research Institute, Toronto, Ontario, Canada, told Medscape Medical News.

In a recent interview with the Associated Press that was published in the *Washington Post*, Dr Jick said his letter was never intended to be used the way it has been. "I'm essentially mortified that that letter to the editor was used as an excuse to do what these drug companies did," he said in the interview.

Taken Out of Context

More than 183,000 deaths from prescription opioids occurred in the United States between 1999 and 2015, report Dr. Juurlink and colleagues.

"The crisis arose in part because physicians were told that the risk of addiction was low when opioids were prescribed for chronic pain," they write.

According to the *Washington Post* story, Dr. Jick's original intent was just to report on short-term use of narcotics in their hospital setting. Their letter was never intended to weigh in on long-term use.

The controversy about the letter, commonly referred to as "Porter and Jick," was discussed in the 2015 book, Dreamland: The True Tale of America's Opiate Epidemic.

That Porter and Jick has been heavily cited "has been known for many years, with many of the citations overstating the conclusion, especially generalizing it to outpatients with chronic pain," said Dr. Juurlink.

"What we wanted to do was examine every citation and characterize how each portrayed the original article," he added. "We suspected we would find the majority would essentially parrot the title ("Addiction Rare in Patients Treated with Narcotics"), and that's exactly what we found."

608 Citations

The investigators identified 608 citations of the original letter "and noted a sizable increase after the introduction of OxyContin…in 1995."

Of these citations, 72.2 percent used the letter as evidence that addiction in opioid-treated patients is rare; 80.8 percent did not mention that the original letter described inpatient findings.

Selected quotes pulled by the researchers from articles citing Porter and Jick include the following:

- "This pain population with no abuse history is literally at no risk for addiction."
- "In reality, medical opioid addiction is very rare."
- "There have been studies suggesting that addiction rarely evolves in the setting of painful conditions."

"This article wasn't even available online until 2010. So until then, all you had was the title and that it was in the New England Journal of Medicine, one of the most prestigious journals in medicine," said Dr. Juurlink.

"I think the title, the source journal, and the fact that it was largely hidden from those who didn't want to make a trip to the library went a long way toward allowing the article to be exploited by individuals seeking to destigmatize opioids for long-term pain. And a lot of those companies had drug-company money behind them."

"A Medical Curiosity"

The original letter is available in the journal's archives, albeit with a new note from the editor at the top warning that it has been "heavily and uncritically cited" in others' arguments that this type of addiction is rare.

Asked if he thinks this new note is enough, Dr. Juurlink said, "I think what you're really asking is if the original letter should be retracted. And the answer to that is no.

"The letter doesn't matter anymore and is now a medical curiosity. Its contribution to the crisis was made long ago. I am glad that the journal has made it open access, and I think adding the note is about all they can do," he said.

"Even if we could snap our fingers and make the letter disappear, the horse has already left the barn."

Dr. Juurlink and two of the other three authors report no relevant financial relationships. The remaining author has received personal fees from Health Quality Ontario outside the submitted work.

N Engl J Med. 2017; 2194-2195.

Follow Deborah Brauser on Twitter: @MedscapeDeb. For more Medscape Neurology news, join us on Facebook and Twitter.

Medscape Medical News © 2017 http://www.medscape.com/ viewarticle/881215?nlid=115577_4503&src=wnl_dne_170607_ mscpedit& uac=152449PR&impID=1363113&faf=1#vp_2

Cite this article: 1980 NEJM Letter the Genesis of the Opioid Crisis?-Medscape-Jun 06, 2017.

A HOLE

You can fill a hole with dirt,
Probably won't even get any on your shirt.

Water could work too,
Wouldn't be that hard to do.

But a hole in your heart,
Can't be filled, no matter how large the cart.

It gets filled with a lot of pain, grief, and sadness,
Which if not checked can drive you to madness.

Be careful what goes in that hole of pain,
If you're looking for your sanity to gain.

There is no special remedy or cure,
God, family, and friends help for sure.

The loss of a child, be it daughter or son,
Leaves a hole that can never be undone.

Father of Nicholas Jordan Di Marco

A LOVE SO STRONG

The death of a child is indescribable you know,
It's a miracle to survive such a devastating blow.

For me what keeps me on my feet,
The love of my son won't let me admit defeat.

While I miss him every single day,
He is by my side so we can help others in every way.

The pain and loss of your leaving,
Makes it worth saving others I'm believing.

Given a choice, on this gamble I would rather not bet,
But there are too many others we must not forget.

My child that was taken too early from me,
Instills the hope that others from this disease can be set free.

Father of Nicholas Jordan Di Marco

ANYONE OUT THERE?

My child has been diagnosed with cancer,
The phone rings faster than I can answer.

Grandma fell and fractured her hip,
Everyone responded so fast you think I used a whip.

And then there was the time mom broke her leg, they swarmed all over
her, till she begged them to leave.

My son has the disease of addiction I swear,
Hello, is there anyone out there?

Father of Nicholas Jordan Di Marco

AN EVIL ROMANCE

When we first met it was not love at first sight,
Your addiction was something I thought I could fight.

Your love was like nothing I ever felt before,
Oh, I wish I never had opened that dark door.

You were created in the depths of hell,
Once tasted I was bound by your spell.

I will always remember our first embrace,
Never to be imitated, just a dream to chase.

Of your bonds I truly wish to break free,
Shackled by self-loathing and misery.

There are some who would from your grasp release me,
While others believe this is just where I should be.

This vile relationship must come to an end,
Your hold on me I must break in the end.

Father of Nicholas Jordan Di Marco

Addiction is defined as a chronic, relapsing brain disease that is characterized by compulsive drug seeking and use, despite harmful consequences. It is considered a brain disease because drugs (believe it or not) change the brain—they change its structure and how it works. These brain changes can be long-lasting and can lead to the harmful behaviors seen in people who use drugs.

ABOUT OPIOID DEPENDENCE

A chronic brain disease, opioid dependence is characterized by cognitive, behavioral, and physiological symptoms in which an individual continues to use opioids despite significant harm to oneself and others. The use of heroin, an illegal opioid drug, and the non-medical use of FDA-approved opioid analgesics, including prescription pain relievers, represents a growing public health problem in the US according to the 2016 US National Survey on Drug Use and Health, nearly two million people aged eighteen or older had an opioid use disorder.

THE "ADDICTION" DEBATE

When a person is addicted, he doesn't control his drug use; his drug use controls him.

When an addict loses the ability to make a rational choice about whether or not to use drugs or alcohol, he or she is addicted.

Addiction is a condition whereby a person experiences an irresistible urge to seek out and use drugs or alcohol despite negative physical and mental consequences.

Addiction is usually accompanied by physical and psychological dependence on the drug and the person suffers withdrawal symptoms when the drug is rapidly decreased or stopped.

Father of Nicholas Jordan Di Marco

A QUESTION

Choice or disease,
Voice your opinions as you please.

But something needs to be done,
If the battle against this epidemic is to be won.

Teach the kids the facts early on year after year,
We need to educate those we hold most dear.

To those that are mixing and dealing this deadly concoction, penalties
should be most severe, the deepest darkest dungeon.

If you think that they deserve to die or in prison they should rot,
We really need to educate you and the whole lot.

Addicts overdose everywhere on the street,
Let's offer Narcan to all that we meet.

Are you trying to stop this circus of addiction?
They just can't find a bed or a place to get in.

Many obstacles to fix this are in our way,
Who will step up to help save the day?

Father of Nicholas Jordan Di Marco

A SILVER LINING

A minute, an hour, or a day,
You've been gone so long, what's there to say?

Just to have you back in my arms to hold,
My soul to the devil I would surely have sold.

The doubts that nag at my brain,
Would drive most people insane.

The unanswered questions that run through my head, looking for ways
to put them to bed.

Your face and memory give me the strength to go on,
So that others may see the coming dawn.

While your body has been taken,
Your spirit has not been forsaken.

My words I speak for others to hear,
Come from the love of you I hold most dear.

I thank you from the bottom of my broken heart; you give me strength
to give others a brand-new start.

Father of Nicholas Jordan Di Marco

THE COST OF ADDICTION

Addiction is a powerful disorder that affects over twenty-three million people in the US alone

1. Addiction costs an estimated $700 billion each year.
2. Over 85 percent of people with alcohol abuse or dependence go untreated.
3. Over two million people in the US abuse prescription pain relievers.
4. An estimated 900,000 people use heroin (an illegal opiate) over 85 percent of people with alcohol abuse or dependence go untreated.

Over two million people in the us abuse prescription pain relievers.

ABOUT ME

I can't believe you lied to me,
Of all the things you could be.

I checked my wallet before I headed out the door,
Looks like some more money is gone just like before.

I don't understand why you can't just quit,
It's not like you can't control this shit.

I am so mad and angry at you,
Why do you do the stuff you do.

I feel so ashamed of what you have done,
Just look at the type of person you have become.

I just found out something about this you see,
It never really was about ME!

Father of Nicholas Jordan Di Marco

ABSENCE OF PRESENCE

Walking down the street moving along,
Out of nowhere I hear your favorite song.

Chest begins to get oh so tight,
Not sure about which is left or right.

How did this all come to be,
Emotions and memories flooding all over me.

Thoughts of you run through my brain,
The pain of loss is nearly driving me insane.

Eyes begin to fill up with tears,
Reruns of "what ifs" and fears.

Trying to catch my breath,
Drained of feelings nothing left.

People always say, "Can't imagine how you feel."
No words to describe, these feelings are so unreal.

The death of a child before their time,
Is just something that words cannot find.

Father of Nicholas Jordan Di Marco

A RESPONSE FROM THE WHITE HOUSE(PRESIDENT BARACK OBAMA)

THE WHITE HOUSE

WASHINGTON

May 1, 2015

Mr. Fred Giuseppe DiMarco
North Olmsted, Ohio

Dear Fred:

Thank you for taking the time to write. I was deeply saddened to learn of the loss of your son and the pain you have experienced.

Too many families are affected by substance use disorders, and our Nation has a responsibility to assist in resolving this public health issue. My Administration is doing everything we can to prevent substance use, help Americans with substance use disorders get treatment, and promote long-term recovery, all while stemming the flow of illicit drugs.

Again, thank you for sharing your son's story. Please know these devastating tragedies motivate my Administration to keep fighting to prevent drug use and its consequences in our communities.

Sincerely,

PETER

Changing the face of addiction!

Prevention

      Education

            Treatment

                Enforcement

                     Recovery

Father of Nicholas Jordan Di Marco

SLAY THE DRAGON, DON'T CHASE IT!

ABYSS

As I stare into the dark abyss,
Thinking about my son who I most surely miss.

A simple man am I,
Who still wants an answer as to why?

Life holds many promises for you and me,
But guarantees are not to be.

How a child can leave this world before a father or mother, Is so unnatural, causing a pain like no other.

We live, laugh, and cry,
Never expecting to have to say goodbye.

We are left with fleeting memories and sorrows,
Wondering how we will get through our tomorrows.

The sun will still rise in the East,
As we must learn to control this painful beast.

We have not been given the reason why they were lost,
But their memories and love we keep no matter what the cost.

Father of Nicholas Jordan Di Marco

OPIOIDS Know the Risks

Rx Drug Drop Box Challenge Pledge

I, _____

will pledge to:

· Practice safe storage techniques with opioid prescriptions.
· Properly dispose unused and old opioid prescriptions.
· Further the conversation about the risks involved with opioid use.

Signature: _____

Date: _____

#KnowTheR_x

ACT

Whether you believe it's a disease or a choice,
Heed my words and listen to my voice.

Innocent people are dying needlessly,
Well over a thousand weekly.

We seemed to be more focused on why,
When we should be more determined not to let them die.

Black or White, Christian or Jew,
Stopping this plague is up to me and you.

It will not be easy, it will not be soon,
But if we fail to act now, how many will go to their doom?

You can give it your all,
Or just make a donation when they call.

But nothing will ever get better,
If we wait for someone else to write the letter.

So, if you want this epidemic to become part of history,
Do it for all of us, for we are all family!

Father of Nicholas Jordan Di Marco

THE FACE OF ADDICTION

Chasing the Dragon is a phrase referring to inhaling vapor from a heated solution of heroin or other opioid. It has become a common metaphor used to describe an addict's constant pursuit of the feeling of their first high.

According to Carrell and many professionals in the field of addiction, heroin is unlike any drug that has plagued families and communities in the past—no one is immune when it comes to heroin addiction.

"I don't care if you wear a tie, if you work in the health care profession, you're a school teacher or a factory worker, I don't care who you are, that is the face of a heroin addict," Carrell said. "That is the sad thing. This drug is not targeting the young or the poor or the depressed, it is targeting people from every walk of life."

Carrell said the age group most commonly seen is between the ages of twenty-five and forty-five. His youngest client being thirteen years old. Often, Carrell says that people are addicted before they ever use heroin the first time.

"We see a lot of clients whose addiction began with prescription pain medication and transitioned into heroin use," Carrell said. "In many cases, the opioid addiction began with pain medication that was actually prescribed to them by a doctor."

Heroin and painkillers belong to the same class of drugs—opioids. Opioids attach to specific molecules called opioid receptors which are found in the nerve cells in the brain, spinal cord, intestines, and other organs, according to Carrell. When painkillers or heroin attach to these receptors, they can decrease the feeling of pain. They can also cause the person to feel relaxed and happy, creating the brain's desire to continue the euphoria.

According to a study by the National Institute of Drug Abuse, eight out of ten people who start using heroin abused painkillers first—often unintentionally.

Often, doctors will cut the dosage or discharge patients without properly weaning them from their pain medication, according to Carrell. Patients who have been using narcotic medication for an extended period of time under a doctor's care, usually for chronic pain, are suddenly faced with insurmountable hurdles to accessing medication they have become addicted to.

"Dr. Brad Lander explains addiction as well as I've ever heard it," Carrell said. "He calls it squirrel logic."

Dr. Brad Lander is the clinical director of addiction psychiatry at Ohio State University's Wexner Medical Center.

"The introduction of addictive substances or behavior to the brain triggers squirrel logic," Lander said. "This sets off a devastating chain reaction and biological transformations."

Lander said as dopamine floods the system; it produces a euphoric feeling that also prevents the body from absorbing the serotonin necessary to modify emotional response.

The brain interprets drugs and alcohol as a new environment and begins to make changes in response, according to Lander. It disconnects and reconnects some nerve cells.

"You've heard people talk about feeling pain in a foot when they don't even have a leg," Lander said. "The reality of the limb is in the brain, not in the limb itself."

According to Lander, it's very similar with addiction. Normally, opioids are the endogenous variety created naturally in the body. Once attached, they send signals to the brain of the opioid effect, which blocks pain, slows breathing, and has a general calming and antidepressing effect. Excessive use of synthetic opioids can cause abnormalities in the cortex of the brain, preventing the brain from being able to distinguish between real and imagined experiences.

Anything that stimulates the reward pathway in the brain is going to be interpreted as something that is necessary for life and needs to be repeated.

"The brain is then convinced it needs heroin the same way it needs food and water," Lander said. "Otherwise, it will die."

ADDICTION AS A DISEASE

Addiction is a complex disease of the brain and body that involves compulsive use of one or more substances despite serious health and social consequences. Addiction disrupts regions of the brain that are responsible for reward, motivation, learning, judgment, and memory. It damages various body systems as well as families, relationships, schools, workplaces, and neighborhoods.

In 2016, there were 64,000 related deaths to opioids, 88,000 related deaths to alcohol, and 480,000 related to cigarette smoking.

I believe it's time to cut the head off of the beast! Maybe more resources should focus on the disease of addiction. A "little" funding from the pharmaceutical companies would go a long way in research.

Just a brokenhearted dad's opinion.

Prevention cannot win the war on drugs.

Education cannot win the war on drugs.

Treatment cannot win the war on drugs.

Enforcement cannot win the war on drugs.

Recovery cannot win the war on drugs.

None of these will work,

ALONE!

HIDDEN IN PLAIN SIGHT

Hey sleepy head, are you going to lay in bed all day,
Seems like just yesterday all you ever wanted to do was play.

You barely touched your plate, you're starting to get thin,
It's your favorite meal (meat loaf and mashed potatoes) you couldn't
wait to dig in.

I haven't seen Josh around anymore,
You two used to trash the house when you wrestled all over the floor.

My mind must be slipping, thought I had an extra $20 in my pocket,
When I leave the house now my last thought is "Did I lock it?"

Sadly, there are many telltale signs here and there,
It's just we didn't know how to read them, not that we didn't care.

Education and prevention go hand in hand,
It will allow you to make better decisions if you understand.

It's hard to open your heart when your mind is closed!

Father of Nicholas Jordan Di Marco

ANNOYING THINGS

I know the phone is not going to ring,
No matter how long I stare at that stupid thing.

I can sit and look at the door,
You're not coming through it like before.

Maybe for the first time your room is neat and clean,
What I wouldn't give for that dirty or messy scene.

The refrigerator door is not left open,
And who do I tell to let the dog in?

Just a few of the simple, irritating things you used to do, that complicate the pain and grief of losing you!

Father of Nicholas Jordan Di Marco

BAD PR

Sixteen years in Vietnam 58 thousand dead,

Opioid deaths will beat that record in one year and put it to bed.

Zika virus spreading like wildfire,

Less than one hundred a year expire.

Planes go up, planes go down,

Less than 400 dead were found.

In 2016 more people left due to an OD,

Than all the car accidents from sea to shining sea.

What is the meaning I'm trying so say,

Too many innocents die from addiction every day.

Why, who, and where the money goes, can't you see,

To those that have the best publicity!

Father of Nicholas Jordan Di Marco

HOW TO RECOGNIZE A HEROIN OVERDOSE

In May of 2018, the Delaware Department of Health and Social services reported two deaths in a twenty-four-hour period as a result of suspected heroin overdose. The agency immediately issued a warning about heroin abuse and the potential risks it carries. In 2018 alone, Delaware reported 106 deaths suspected to be heroin overdose-related.

Your loved one might be abusing heroin right under your nose without you being aware of it. Sometimes, addicts go to great lengths to conceal their drug abuse habits. At any rate, it is possible to observe a few clues before the situation becomes hopeless. If you notice the following physical symptoms in a loved one, it may be that they are overdosing on heroin:

- Limp body
- Vomiting
- Inability to speak
- Low blood pressure
- Slow heartbeat
- Slow breathing
- Extremely pale face
- Blue or purple lips or fingernails
- Difficulty waking up from sleep

Few people who overdose on fentanyl-laced heroin make it to the emergency room. If you suspect that your loved one has overdosed on heroin, call 911 immediately.

BREAD CRUMBS

Even as a child while riding his bike,
Trouble with the law, he did not like.

PSR for all of God's children,
Not for you, you didn't fit in.

Teachers taught the golden rule,
When you didn't listen, their anger you would fuel.

The principal and superintendent said they wanted what was best for you,
While they did nothing to help or understand is the truth.

Caught by the men in blue, come clean and we'll let you go,
That never happened, how were you to know?

Counselor said get a prescription for Narcan,
Doctor said no that's not going to happen.

Ignorance, pride or shame, where or who to place the blame,
Too late for some but let's not have others fall to the same.

Father of Nicholas Jordan Di Marco

THE STREET COST OF HEROIN

How much does heroin cost on the street?

The price of heroin depends upon a number of different factors—including the type of heroin, how available the drug is to the public at a given time, and how the heroin is "cut" and processed.

The average cost of a single dose (0.1 g) of heroin purchased on the street has been reported as approximately $15–$20 in the US state of Ohio.

The heroin price per gram depends upon its purity and the availability of the drug in the area at that given time.

Someone with a "hard-core" heroin habit may pay $150–$200 per day in order to support his or her habit.

The reason for such a high daily spending habit has its roots in the nature of heroin addiction. As individuals become more dependent on the drug, they build tolerance to it—meaning that it takes more and more heroin to get high. This leads to an expensive habit—and the constant threat of overdose.

Lost to overdose 72K (2017)

Add two parents-144K
Add four grandparents 288K
Add other family and friends?

And you think it only affects the addict?

Over the past decade, out-of-state drug companies shipped 20.8 million prescription painkillers to two pharmacies four blocks apart in a Southern West Virginia town with 2,900 people, according to a congressional committee investigating the opioid crisis.

Walmart offers kits to turn leftover opioids into useless gel

Walmart (WMT) says it's giving away a tool to help curtail the opioid epidemic: free packets that turn the addictive painkillers into a useless gel.

The retail giant announced Wednesday that it will provide the packets free with opioid prescriptions filled at its 4,700 US pharmacies.

The small packets, made by DisposeRX, contain a powder that is poured into prescription bottles. When mixed with warm water, the powder turns the pills into a biodegradable gel that can be thrown in the trash. Research has shown that surgery patients often end up with leftover opioid painkillers and store the drugs improperly at home.

The brain tries to file the pain of the loss away

But the heart keeps getting in our way.

Father of Nicholas Jordan Di Marco

HOMECOMING

As I looked down upon the earth, I noticed your pain was so great,
For I wanted to relieve you of this burden and take you quickly to
heaven's gate.

I know you tried to beat this evil that had its horrible grip on you,
So many different times you had tried, you didn't know what more to do.

To take you away from family and friends some may not think is right,
With so much pain and sorrow, I thought it was best to end the fight.

Placed in my arms and under my wing,
I will remove your sadness and now you may hear the angels sing.

To have your life stop so young and short may seem quite cold,
Sadly, life was not meant to always let us grow old.

It's a bittersweet thing to be taken from your precious family and
friends,
Who will surely cherish and miss you until the bitter end.

For I could not bear any longer your pain and sorrow,
As you were brought to heaven today instead of tomorrow.

Father of Nicholas Jordan Di Marco

HOW CAN YOU TELL IF YOUR CHILD IS USING DRUGS OR ALCOHOL?

Teens are known to have mood swings. However, some behavior may indicate more serious issues, such as abuse of drugs and alcohol. Here are some of the warning signs of drug use.

Problems at school

- Frequently forgetting homework.
- Missing classes or skipping school.
- Disinterest in school or school activities.
- A drop in grades.

Physical signs

- Lack of energy and motivation.
- Red eyes and cheeks or difficulty focusing (alcohol use)
- Red eyes and constricted pupils (marijuana use)
- A strange burn on your child's mouth or fingers (smoking something [possibly heroin] through a metal or glass pipe)
- Chronic nosebleeds (cocaine abuse)

Neglected appearance

- Lack of interest in clothing, grooming, or appearance is not normal. (Teenagers are usually very concerned about how they look.)

Changes in behavior

- Teenagers enjoy privacy but be aware of excessive attempts to be alone.
- Exaggerated efforts not to allow family members into their rooms.

- Not letting you know where they go with friends or whom they go with.
- Breaking curfew without a good excuse.
- Changes in relationships with family.

Changes in friends

- No longer friends with childhood friends.
- Seems interested in hanging out with older kids.
- Acts secretive about spending time with new friends.

Money issues

- Sudden requests for money without a good reason.
- Money stolen from your wallet or from safe places at home.
- Items gone from your home. (May be sold to buy drugs.)

Specific smells

- Odor of marijuana, cigarettes, or alcohol on teen's breath, on clothing, in the bedroom, or in the car.

Drug paraphernalia

- Finding items in your child's room, backpack, or car related to drug use.

BUY IN

The cop on the beat,
Is doing what he can to keep drugs off the street.

Parents searching for answers, doing their best,
They just don't know the right questions or answers to the test.

First responders have added Narcan to their arsenal,
Trying to save as many lives as possible.

Schools that just used to show them the door,
Are looking at different avenues more than before.

Recovery and sober living houses are opening up left and right,
We all know more beds are needed to win this fight.

Churches who for so long looked the other way,
Are now taking a good look and want to join in the fray.

All these and more are needed if this war we want to win,
Most importantly we need the addicts to join in!

Father of Nicholas Jordan Di Marco

CHOICE OR FATE

Life was never fair,
Death just doesn't care.

Good things happen to bad people,
Bad things happen to good people.

You get up and go about town,
Never having a clue what's about to go down.

The plan in your head is to stay ahead of the game,
But shit happens and you're ready to go insane.

So, take what you know,
Go with the flow.

You will always have questions and looking up to the sky, Asking the
worn-out question of why.

Some things we will never know,
Like why did you have to go!

Father of Nicholas Jordan Di Marco

I CHOOSE

To cry in front of a crowd,
I'm really not that proud.

To speak his name,
I'm not afraid of stigma or shame.

To share a drink or two,
I'm not staying blue.

Our family lost a son and a brother,
I choose not to let this happen to another

Father of Nicholas Jordan Di Marco

HOW WAS YOUR DAY

Law enforcement says, "Had to arrest a kid on an outstanding theft warrant. He's going to jail, no detox or bail."

First responders say, "Had to use Narcan six times on an overdose victim this morning passed out in a car. I've never seen it this bad so far."

Mom says, "I worry to death that something bad is going to happen to him, these drugs are pure evil, the darkest sin."

The neighbor says, "No one put a gun to her head, it was her choice, it's not my fault if she ends up dead."

The addict says, "Yesterday was really bad, dope sick and drug court, but today I'm getting help, looking good, got plenty of support."

Five different answers from five different people. Oh my—the saddest part is they could all be talking about the same guy!

Father of Nicholas Jordan Di Marco

TREATMENT VS. INCARCERATION

Every eighteen seconds, an American is arrested for drug possession (Centers for Disease Control 2010). The United States has spent over $14 billion for drug control, of which about 66 percent went toward incarceration, border control, international production reduction, and other supply-side activities; and only about 32 percent went to prevention and treatment (Office of National Drug Control Policy 2008). Approximately 70 percent of state prisoners are there for drug-related offenses (Petteruti and Walsh 2008).

Basically, the US is wasting billions of dollars by incarcerating drug addicts who are arrested for drug offenses as this becomes a revolving door, if the addict remains an addict. What it should be doing is insisting on treatment for non-violent offenders. This would drastically reduce crime, re-incarceration, and rearrests while increasing savings because there would be fewer prisoners.

If someone is arrested for possession of an illegal substance, once they are arrested, they sometimes sit in prison for a long period of time. We know they are not getting any real treatment for their addiction while in prison. So they complete their sentence and are released back into the community. Why are we then surprised when they start using again, inevitably winding up back in prison? They haven't confronted any of their issues, made any kind of amends with their family and friends to rebuild their relationships to hopefully have a support system, nor gotten down to the root of why they use drugs in the first place. And they, most likely, return to the same drug-using environment from which they had been arrested.

People use drugs as an attempt to solve some problem they have. It allows them to feel numb and not have to confront the problem. Without helping them figure out how to solve these problems in a different way other than using drugs, they are going to revert back to the solution that has worked for them in the past, which is using drugs. It's a vicious cycle and is costing our country billions spending hard earned taxpayer's money.

Most importantly and in addition to that, these are human beings who have an addiction. People who need help. They aren't bad people.

They are our family members, our friends, and our neighbors. They deserve a chance to change in order to become contributing members of society, not just be put away to rot in isolation. Sure, they have made some bad decisions and some questionable choices in their lives; I'm not perfect either. I've never used drugs. However, I would hope that if it were me, I would be given at least the opportunity to turn my life around. I think it's important to remember who they were before they started using because, I guarantee you, they were completely different—the drugs change them.

My point is, with the rate people are dying, as well as the rate we are locking people up, we need to make a change. What we are doing is not working. We need to be giving more support to the treatment centers and insisting treatment for nonviolent offenders. With successful treatment, people will return to their work, family, and community obligations and go on to live happy healthy lives. Isn't that what we should strive for?

I WANT TO BE

When I was young, I wanted to be a rap singer,
Gold chains, diamond rings on every finger.

A doctor healing the sick,
I figured that would do the trick.

Man could I carry the ball,
The only thing I thought about was playing in the fall.

Somehow, someway things just didn't work out the way I planned,
Not sure when, not sure how I still don't really understand.

The last thing in the world that I thought would happen to me,
Is to turn into an addict you see.

When it came time to decide what you want to be when you grow up
list,
Addicted to drugs wasn't anywhere on my mind if you get my gist.

It was never something we were looking to become,
Watching our world fall apart while coming undone.

Stop and take a deep look into the addict that you meet,
At some time, anyone could be in that seat.

Father of Nicholas Jordan Di Marco

COLLATERAL BEAUTY

My heart's been broken, torn to shreds,
A parent's worst nightmare has come to bed.

I met a mother the other day,
She hugged and kissed me and was so happy I must say.

When you lose a child to this dreaded disease of addiction,
The hard-cold facts are stranger than fiction.

Her daughter was pregnant, using and heading toward death's door,
Made some calls, the cavalry answered that's for sure.

The loss is great, agony and grief,
How you can survive is beyond belief.

The daughter and child are healthy and clean,
The look on Grandma's face is something to be seen.

Horrible things happen to people like me and you,
But there is a lot of good in this world that much is true.

Father of Nicholas Jordan Di Marco

COUNTDOWN TO A MELTDOWN

I got the dreaded call today,
They told me that you had gone away.

While the brain started to process the information,
The heart went into palpitations.

Words came out of people's mouths,
I'm sure they were words of comfort, no doubt.

Feeling empty, strained and sanity going down the drain,
Yet so full of sorrow, grief, and pain.

So now where do I go from here?
The love for you I'll hold most dear.

Father of Nicholas Jordan Di Marco

JUST ONCE MORE

Just once more,
I would like to see you walk through the door.

How my heart would sing,
To be home praying for that phone to ring.

Just to hear you scream at me,
Why don't you just let me be?

You used to make me so mad,
Now I'm just sad.

How about one more time,
For you to step out of line.

One more sleepless night,
Checking your room in a fright.

While there were some difficult times up till the end,
Just once more I want to hold you again!

Father of Nicholas Jordan Di Marco

Most demographic groups are increasingly using heroin and other drugs.

During the past decade, heroin use has increased across the United States among men and women, most age groups, and all income levels, with some of the greatest increases occurring in demographic groups that have had historically lower rates of heroin use, according to a new Vital Signs report.

A wider variety of people are using heroin. Rates remained highest among males, eighteen-to twenty-five-year-olds, people with annual incomes less than $20,000, people living in urban areas, and people with no health insurance or those enrolled in Medicaid. However, rates increased significantly across almost all study groups. They doubled among women and more than doubled among non-Hispanic whites.

- It is common for people who use heroin to use other drugs. Nearly all (96 percent) people who reported heroin use also reported using at least one other drug in the past year. More than half (61 percent) used at least three other drugs. Prescription opioid painkiller abuse or dependences was the strongest risk factor for heroin abuse or dependence; 45 percent of people who used heroin also abused or were dependent on prescription opioid painkillers in the past year.
- As heroin abuse or dependence increased, so have heroin-related overdose deaths. From 2002 through 2013, the rate of heroin-related overdose deaths nearly quadrupled.

CHOICE

To those that think drug addiction is a choice,
Please listen to my words, heed my voice.

Have you ever seen your son being handcuffed and led off to jail?
Then scrambling and begging for money to make bail?

Your spouse has lost the will to live,
You're exhausted with nothing left to give.

You have an opinion that much is true,
But without the facts you haven't a clue.

Learn the ins and outs about the disease,
Before you open your mouth, please.

Until you've held your lifeless son in your arms,
Then you can come before me and stand.

Father of Nicholas Jordan Di Marco

CRIME AND PUNISHMENT

If you can't do the time,
Don't do the crime.

Heard that so many times before,
Once more and I'll bang my head on the door.

While I'm not advocating for a free pass,
Some issues are just not clear as glass.

The drug addict who gets put away,
Do they really get better that way?

To put them behind bars a lot of money is spent,
Cheaper and advantageous to rehab I'll bet.

Sitting rotting in a cell,
No sure how that is going to make them well.

Prisons are already full to the brim,
The violent offenders, let's keep them in.

Father of Nicholas Jordan Di Ma

WHAT ARE THE TEN MOST COMMON SIGNS AND SYMPTOMS OF DRUG USE AND ADDICTION?

If you or someone you love is addicted to drugs or alcohol, they could exhibit a few or all of the following signs and symptoms:

- *Cravings.* People may experience intense urges or cravings for the drug as their addiction develops.
- *Physical dependence.* Physical dependence to drugs can develop as people grow accustomed to the persistent presence and influence of the substance. The changes in physiology that accompany this process leave people feeling badly or functioning sub-optimally when the drug is no longer in the system.
- *Tolerance.* Over time and with prolonged use, people can build up a tolerance to the drug; meaning they need more of the drug to achieve the desired effects.
- *Withdrawal symptoms.* Some people experience withdrawal symptoms when they attempt to stop using abruptly or when they wean themselves off the drug over a period of time. This is the presence of a withdrawal syndrome indicates that physiologic dependence is at play.
- *Poor judgement.* When an individual is addicted to drugs, he or she may do anything to obtain more, including risky behaviors such as stealing, lying, engaging in unsafe sexual activity, selling drugs, or crimes that could land the person in jail.
- *Drug-seeking.* People may spend excessive amounts of time and energy finding and getting their drug of choice.
- *Financial trouble.* People may spend large amounts of money, drain their bank accounts, and go outside their budgets in order to get the drug. This is a major red flag.

- *Neglect responsibilities.* When people choose using or getting the drug over meeting work or personal obligations, this is a classic sign of addiction.
- *Develop unhealthy friendships.* When people start using new substances, they may spend time with others who have similar habits. They may hang out with a new group of people who may encourage unhealthy habits.
- *Isolate.* Alternatively, they may withdraw and isolate themselves, hiding their drug use from friends and family. Some reasons for this may include perceived stigma or increased depression, anxiety, or paranoia as a result of their drug addiction.

The opioid epidemic, which has taken hundreds of thousands of lives, has also taken a massive toll on the economy. The total economic cost of the crisis reached at least $631 billion from 2015 to 2018, an analysis found.

Over the past decade, out-of-state drug companies shipped 20.8 million prescription painkillers to two pharmacies four blocks apart in a Southern West Virginia town with 2,900 people, according to a congressional committee investigating the opioid crisis.

THE HOLY PROFIT

Blouse a little open, skirt a little short,
Big smile, for this doctor I must court.

My presentation needs to be smooth,
Bat the eyes, make my move.

This new drug is the latest and the greatest,
It has passed all the trials and clinical tests.

The more prescriptions you write,
Will pack your bags, and book the flight.

Oh, by the way, the higher the dosage you recommend,
The better your bank account is in the end.

Shade the truth, twist the facts for us,
Sell the product, make the quarterly bonus.

Big Pharma looks to capitalize on a need,
Sadly, all just for common greed.

The doctor in white with all his charm,
Seems to forget "you shouldn't do harm!"

Father of Nicholas Jordan Di Marco

COMING TO TERMS

I lost my son some time ago,
More like taken from me I would say so.

No one thinks it can happen to me,
It's always someone else you see.

You're the loving parent full of anger and frustration,
Trying to do your best with ignorance, stigma, and no education.

You yell, holler, and scream in vain,
Not having a clue what it's done to his brain.

Denial and embarrassment hold you back,
From making the best plan of attack.

The word is slowly getting out,
The disease of addiction is what it's about.

At one time a choice it may be,
But once drawn in it's not that easy.

My advice to those that still battle this affliction, learn all that you can
for recovery to come to fruition.

Father of Nicholas Jordan Di Marco

THE OPIOID THIEF

I come with promises of sweet relief.
I am called the opioid thief.

Want to do just a little for some fun,
I'll take from you everything under the sun.

The relationship with Mom and Dad,
That will become the worst you ever had.

The girlfriend in your arms you used to love to hold, after the stealing
and lying it's going to grow cold.

Your job that you liked so well,
It's gone, your boss has told you to go to hell.

The last thing I will take from you after all the strife,
Will plain and simply be your life!

Father of Nicholas Jordan Di Marco

Letter to the Ohio State Representative

4/24/15

Dear Mr. Schumann, Ward 3

The results show the rate of death from heroin overdose nearly quadrupled, from 0.7 deaths per 100,000 people in the year 2000, to 2.7 deaths per 100,000 people in 2013. But the steepest rise occurred between 2010 and 2013, when the rate of death from heroin overdose increased 37 percent, compared with rising just 6 percent over the decade before, according to the report from the Centers for Disease Control and Prevention (CDC).

I would like to know what is being done to address the cause rather than the symptoms of the heroin epidemic that is growing at an ever-alarming rate in the United States.

- Heroin dealers receive probation rather than jail time and/or stiff monetary penalties more often than not
- Heroin dealers who put "fentanyl" (a leading cause of Heroin related deaths/Overdose) suffer no additional legal recourse
- Heroin addicted people are filling up our already overcrowded jails
- Heroin addicted people are increasing our health care costs
- Heroin addicted people are increasing the crime rate (theft & burglaries)

The vast number of people affected by this epic tragedy is growing at an exponential rate & needs to be addressed.

PS: I lost my 18-year-old son on 3/9/15 to a fentanyl laced heroin drug overdose.

Sincerely,

Fred G. Di Marco

ENOUGH

Every morning I have to answer the face in the mirror,
The same questions with solutions no clearer.

Why didn't you just throw him out?
Should have kept him closer without a doubt.

Jail would have been the cure for him,
The things he's done to get high were a sin.

Find the cash get her into recovery fast,
It's not that bad she thinks it won't last.

Did I do enough?
Or was I just too tough?

Over and over I hear my voice,
Did you make the right choice?

The best answer I can possibly give,
All my decisions were made from my love within.

Father of Nicholas Jordan Di Marco

CHOICES

A choice has been made,
The cards have been played.

You decided to give it a shot,
Even though what was in it you knew not.

You tore your knee on second base,
The good doctor gave you something to get back in the race.

It won't happen to me, I'm smarter than the others,
That's funny, then why are there so many dead brothers?

Anxiety, depression, or boredom,
It doesn't matter where your decision came from.

Once you get trapped in this maze,
It's no longer a phase.

Three paths you may take,
Jail, recovery, or death for goodness sake.

May your decision be true,
If you know what is best for you.

Father of Nicholas Jordan Di Marco

I WANT A DREAM

I want a dream that one day on the rolling hills of Ohio, sons of former addicts and the sons of former addict haters will be able to sit down together at the table of brotherhood.

I want a dream that one day even the state of Ohio, a state with vast numbers of innocent lives lost daily to the chronic brain disease of addiction, will be transformed into an oasis of recovery and treatment.

I want a dream that my children will one day live in a nation where they will not be judged by their addiction but by the content of their character. I want a dream... I want a dream that one day in Maine with its vicious stigma of addiction, law enforcement not willing to use Narcan, one day right there in Maine addicts and nonaddicts will be able to join hands as sisters and brothers.

I want a dream today... I want a dream that one day every valley shall be exalted, every hill and mountain shall be made low. The rough places will be made plain, and the crooked places will be made straight. And the glory of the Lord shall be revealed, and all flesh shall see it together. This is our hope. This is the faith that I go back to the world with. With this faith, we will be able to hew out of the mountain of despair a stone of hope. With this faith, we will be able to transform the jangling discords of our nation into a beautiful symphony of brotherhood. With this faith, we will be able to educate together, to find treatment together, to get recovery together, to stand up for those with the disease of addiction together, knowing that we will be free one day.

Father of Nicholas Jordan Di Marco and MLK

PRESCRIPTION DRUG DISPOSAL BOXES TO BE INSTALLED AT CUYAHOGA COMMUNITY COLLEGE CAMPUSES

Karen Farkas
cleveland.com kfarkas@cleveland.com

CLEVELAND, Ohio-Cuyahoga Community College will install disposal boxes for prescription drugs on campus to provide secure locations for the community to throw away unused medications.

Tri-C campus police and the Cuyahoga County Sheriff's Department collaborated on the disposal-box project in response to the region's ongoing opioid crisis. The Sheriff's Office will be in charge of emptying the boxes and discarding the drugs.

The disposal boxes will be in the student services buildings at Eastern Campus in Highland Hills and Metropolitan Campus in Cleveland; the Galleria at Western

Campus in Parma; and the lobby of Westshore Campus in Westlake.

The boxes should be installed by the end of the month.

"We are installing these boxes to help protect our college and the community," Tri-C Police Lt. Thomas McMillan said in a news release. "We want individual community members, students, faculty and staff to have a safe place to dispose of unwanted prescription medication."

The white metal boxes allow for the disposal of any solid medication, such as pills, capsules, or skin patches. Needles, liquids, and biohazardous materials should not be left in the boxes.

MORE FACTS

Functions of Dopamine—What Is Dopamine?

Dopamine is a molecule that our body produces naturally, and it's the substance that's behind our dreams and biggest secrets. Dopamine means lust, love, infidelity, motivation, attention, femininity, learning, and addiction.

Dopamine is like a chemical messenger in the brain, which is technically known as a neurotransmitter and is responsible for sending signals from the central nervous system. It is what allows information to be passed from one neuron to another.

Dopamine's effects on the brain depend on a few different factors and is influenced by the other types of neurons that it's combined with. Scientists originally thought that this substance was related to real pleasure, the pleasure that we've experienced. However, it's recently been argued that dopamine is more related to anticipatory pleasure and motivation.

Functions of Dopamine and Addictions

For most addiction-causing drugs, they work by targeting the dopamine neurotransmitters in your brain. Drugs like cocaine and amphetamines inhibit the re-uptake of dopamine in each synapse available. What this means is that usually, a synapse is composed of a neuron that is releasing a specific neurotransmitter and another neuron that is receiving the said neurotransmitter with a gap between the two called a synaptic cleft. Neurons communicate with each other through different means, and one of these involves the process of reuptake. Reuptake refers to what happens after the neurotransmitter is released from the first neuron. In order to recycle the neurotransmitter, the first neuron will absorb what it has released after the neurotransmitter's job has completed and then re-use it again when necessary. Re-uptake also controls the amount of the said neurotransmitter available for the brain's usage so that an excessive amount is not present.

So, because cocaine and amphetamines inhibit the reuptake of dopamine, they are stopping neurons from reabsorbing the used dopamine, so it stays present in the brain for longer periods of time. This extra dopamine causes one to experience heightened feelings of pleasure and addiction in wanting more of the drug.

Heroin

Drug

Heroin, also known as diamorphine among other names, is an opioid most commonly used as a recreational drug for its euphoric effects. It is used medically in several countries to relieve pain or in opioid replacement therapy. It is typically injected, usually into a vein, but it can also be smoked, snorted, or inhaled. The onset of effects is usually rapid and lasts for a few hours.

Chemical formula: $C_{21}H_{23}NO_5$

DON'T ASK, DON'T TELL

"How are you feeling?" they ask.
You don't really want to know, I think.

As I continue my tasks,
My grief and sorrow have put me on the brink.

He's in a better place they say,
I would have it a different way.

Or, it's God's will,
While my heart pays the bill.

I am the daytime nightmare of folks,
Who most could not fathom or cope?

I use my pain and grief,
In hopes of bringing someone else relief.

Father of Nicholas Jordan Di Marco

DEATH WALKS THE STREETS

Whether its needles, powder, or pills,
One or all three will surely kill.

The man on the street has a plan,
And that's to sell you as much as he can.

You're too smart to be taken advantage of,
Just give me that stuff that I falsely love.

He'll sell it to you fast, he'll sell it to you slow,
Just as long as he can watch the money flow.

He cares not if you live or die,
Just as long as he can look fly.

We beg, plead, cry, and pray
That you will live another day.

Father of Nicholas Jordan Di Marco

EMPTY

I wear your ring,
Yet I don't feel a thing.

Your clothes if they fit,
Can't help me a bit.

I put your picture in a frame,
Still can't get it through my brain.

Maybe a stone with your name,
Will help to lessen the blame.

The one thing that I know to the core,
You will no longer be walking in the door.

Father of Nicholas Jordan Di Marco

DIFFERENT PATHS

The addict wanders the street,
Looking for shelter and some food to eat.

Mom is home alone,
Sitting crying by the phone.

Dad turns his head and looks away,
Because he doesn't know what to do or say.

The cop who cruises the street,
Is tired of all the ODs and is mentally beat.

Each and every one,
Is going in the wrong direction.

Somehow someday,
We need to be going the same way.

Father of Nicholas Jordan Di Marco

FAME OR FOLLY

I've been asked to speak at a rally or two,
It's something that I've become accustomed to.

Families who have lost a loved one may contact me,
They are not sure where to go or who to see.

Interview with the news, radio, or TV,
I'll talk to anyone willing to hear me.

Find an addict a safe place to stay,
What can I do to get them out of harm's way?

Sometimes it puts me in the spotlight,
And it doesn't always feel quite right.

Why do I and others do this for our fellow brother,
Simply because what happened to us should never happen to another!

Father of Nicholas Jordan Di Marco

FOREVER 18

I was there to watch your mother give birth,
The price of admission it truly was worth.

I got to watch you stand on your own two feet,
No longer crawling on all fours was pretty neat.

When I brought home your very first car,
I didn't know you could jump so far.

Now I will never know,
What career path you would have chosen to go.

Or see you bursting at the seams,
To tell me you found the love of your dreams.

Maybe the child you could have brought into this light, Telling me
how you are gonna get this one right.

These things are only now part of my affliction,
Taken away by the disease of addiction.

Father of Nicholas Jordan Di Marco

FOREVER BROKEN

Got a broken windshield the other day,
They filled it with resin and made it go away.

Duct tape can fix almost anything,
From a tear to a broken swing.

Mom's favorite vase,
A little super glue and back in the case.

Even metal can be soldered or fixed with a weld,
Just remember to let it cool before it is held.

Now the heart, that is quite different you see,
Once broken it can never really be.

The loss of a loved one,
Is just something that can't be undone!

Father of Nicholas Jordan Di Marco

FOREVER IMMORTAL

Funny how our memories can play tricks on us,
Know your friends address but still miss the bus.

An anniversary or birthday was today,
Forgot again, don't know what to say.

What was the name of that restaurant we liked so well?
It's on the tip of my tongue, oh hell.

Many things our brains try to process,
Some stay, some go who's to guess.

The one thing that will always be,
The memory of my son who left me.

The good, the bad, happy, or sad will not wane,
Forever immortal the memories embedded in my brain.

Father of Nicholas Jordan Di Marco

GONE

Went to a funeral just today,s
Does anyone really know what to say?

Gone too fast, too young and much too soon,
I don't think there was a dry eye in the room.

Mom was a basket case,
The loss of her son all over her face.

Dad held the line, kept his head held high,
A dad to the end, so sad he never got to say goodbye.

Everyday families and friends gather round,
For the task of putting loved ones in the ground.

A simple question I ask of you,
If you could, what would or could you do?

Dedicated to the family of Josh Kivon

HATE

There are many things that I do not like,
A child's cry when they fall off a bike.

A few things I truly hate to see,
Bullies, rapists, and pedophiles are three.

But the top of my list there is only one,
That is the disease of addiction.

While normally a quiet man am I,
If heroin were human, I would stab it in the eye.

My emotions I try to keep on an even keel,
Opioids to the ax I would make them kneel.

A poison it is, deadly as sin,
How it has destroyed innocents where do you begin.

If only you could feel so I could cause you pain,
Maybe it would give some small pleasure I would gain.

Sadly, you are not alive to feel my sorrow, Because of you my son has
no tomorrow.

Father of Nicholas Jordan Di Marco

HEROIN

You broke my heart,
But not my will.

You stole my child,
Yet I hold his memory still.

Your reign of death has to stop,
Far too many lives have been wasted.

The false promises that you make,
Come to pass once you've been tasted.

Know this here and now,
I will not rest, I know your worth.

I will fight until I breathe no more,
Until you are gone from this earth.

Father of Nicholas Jordan Di Marco

HISTORY LESSON

A doctor's visit to ease the pain,
How many prescriptions are written in vain?

Oxys, Percs, Vics, Opioids of your choice,
Were given out as long as you had a voice.

The pill mills finally got shut down,
Soon after Heroin moved into town.

Cheap and strong the vacuum got filled,
Tragic how many were getting killed.

Heroin now has a backseat,
Fentanyl is now the new treat.

Heroin on steroids is the lore,
Sadly, more are dying than before.

A new player is entering the game,
Carfentanil is its name.

It has no use for man or woman,
Just one spec and you are done!

Father of Nicholas Jordan Di Marco

HOPES AND DREAMS*

Dedicated to my Aunt Olivia

I search the faces of strangers, as I pass them on the street, Hoping to
see a resemblance of you, so strong and sweet.

Your favorite shirt while I see it worn by another,
Sends a quick shiver and my heart goes a flutter.

My nose takes in the scent of your favorite cologne, when I look
around, I'm still alone.

A truck like the one you drove comes down the street,
My mind plays tricks and puts you in the seat.

Sights and sounds remind me of you every day,
As I try to keep hold of you in every way.

Father of Nicholas Jordan Di Marco

HOPES AND FALSE DREAMS

I really want to walk through that door,
I've thought about it a thousand times before.

I got to get out of the mix,
But all I can think about is the next fix.

Smiles and happy faces will greet me when I enter,
But how does it work when I falter?

The puzzle and the maze are so confusing just to get in,
No beds today, tomorrow we'll try again.

Leave me alone, can't you see,
I just want to be wrapped in that warm blanket of ecstasy.

I know it's not real, it's a sham,
I'm just holding on the best I can.

Father of Nicholas Jordan Di Marco

I GAVE, YOU TOOK

I gave a wedding vow,
Crushed dreams and hopes you would allow.

You took a child sick with a disease,
Gave him false promises and did with him what you pleased.

I've had many sleepless nights,
You pit us against each other for many agonizing fights.

You took a person from a home,
Left them in the streets to die alone.

I gave with all the love in my heart,
Only to be left with it broken and torn apart.

You let greed overcome goodwill,
Wanting only your pockets to fill.

I gave my son what I thought was best,
Because of you I laid him to rest.

Father of Nicholas Jordan Di Marco

HOW

How can my heart be so empty, and my grief so full?

My memories become faded and old, while my blood runs cold.

The innocent laughter of a child, makes my tears run wild.

Do we recover, knowing you will never have a lover?

How did this become, your death from HEROIN?

Father of Nicholas Jordan Di Marco

I KNOW

I know a lot about opioids/heroin,
Like when and where it's from.

How to administer the Narcan spray,
It's used somewhere every day.

About different types of treatment,
From tough love, faith-based, or just plain vent.

Many still believe it's a choice,
That we need a louder voice.

What I don't know, is what to do,
About how badly I'm missing you!

Father of Nicholas Jordan Di Marco

I REMEMBER

The day you were born,
When my life as a dad began to form,

Growing up from a boy to a young man,
And I thinking I was doing the best I can,

Crawling on the ground on all four,
To running around all night coming in at four.

Trying to teach you right from wrong,
While you were blasting your favorite song.

The anger, frustration, pain, and shame,
Just not knowing where to place the blame.

But what I remember most,
Is that now you have become a ghost.

Father of Nicholas Jordan Di Marco

I TRIED

From a crawl to a walk, or a gaga to talk,

I'm here to teach you to ride a bike,
Or go for a nice long hike.

Another parent-teacher meeting,
I'd rather be watching the game and/or eating.

As parents we do what we do,
Because it's supposed to be good for you.

You're in trouble with the law again,
Let me go and talk to them.

Judges, lawyers, and POs,
Do they really understand your woes?

With these two hands I can tear down a wall with ease, but I couldn't
protect you from your disease.

I've been told so many times that you can't save them all, That it really
isn't my call.

I was only trying to save the one,
And that was you, my loving son!

Father of Nicholas Jordan Di Marco

I WAS HE

Back when my child was struck by his addiction,
As a dad I was embarrassed he was my son.

Not understanding the grip, the disease had a hold on him, Why to
this temptation would he give in.

The lying and stealing from family and friends,
I had no tolerance and demanded it must end.

Many hard choices and decisions I made during these tough days,
Hoping tough love would end his using ways.

Ignorance and stigma were a partner in my plan,
To teach my son how to be a man.

I loved my son with all my heart,
But my brain didn't have the facts from the start.

I did everything I thought was best for him to recover,
My child I did not want to suffer.

I have a completely different understanding of my son now you see,
when I look in the mirror and see the old me.

Open your eyes and ears to learn as much as you can,
For making the best decisions on how to treat this disease that effects
all man.

Father of Nicholas Jordan Di Marco

"I"

I could lay in bed all day,

I could have nothing to say.
4

What if I just let it go?

What if I kept it on the down low?
4

Then you wouldn't know how I feel,

Even though the pain is so unreal.
4

Why do I do what I do?

Simple, it's because I miss you.

Father of Nicholas Jordan Di Marco

IF ONLY

Mom, if only I could turn back time,
Would our lives be different, yours and mine?

If only the chronic disease of addiction had a fix,
Then so many like I wouldn't be in this mix.

If only knowledge replaced the current stigma,
Maybe so many deaths wouldn't be such an enigma.

If only we place more in treatment and reform,
Than jail which has become the norm.

If only we provided the tools of prevention,
Rather than looks of condemnation.

If only we made Narcan more available for all,
To be there when someone gets the call.

If only more of these were made known,
Maybe I wouldn't have to have written this poem.

Father of Nicholas Jordan Di Marco

IGNORANCE

I have two eyes but cannot see,
The addiction that lies in front of me.

A pair of ears I use to hear,
Become deaf from words due to fear.

The chains of pride and shame,
Bind me to place the blame.

Listen and learn,
So as not to crash and burn.

Father of Nicholas Jordan Di Marco

INSTRUCTIONS

You're sixteen, time to bone up, read the book,
Get your temp, it will be off the hook.

ACT or SAT tests coming up, need a high score,
Take the prep tests, study so you can score more.

Want to bake a cake,
Read the back of the box so you don't make a mistake.

Almost anything you want to say or do,
Somewhere there is a "how to."

What I find most sad, that one of the most important things to do,
When being a mom or dad, raising kids you don't have a clue.

There is no school to graduate from or test to take,
For your children the best decisions you hope you make.

Father of Nicholas Jordan Di Marco

LEARNING CURVE

What do you mean you can't quit,
It's a state of mind, just get over it.

If you know what is good for you,
You will do what I tell you to do.

What's that, I don't understand?
Just stop and be a man.

Too late, I spoke out of line,
I never bothered to take the time.

I thought I was doing what was best for you,
Not understanding that I didn't have a clue.

While there is no one way to recover,
The best odds to beat this is to learn and discover.

Father of Nicholas Jordan Di Marco

LESSON IN HISTORY

Over 100 years ago, 2 Bayer scientists thought they had the cure, Heroin was created to stop the opium and morphine that's for sure.

For many years it stayed down low,
Only the rich or poor chose there to go.

Purdue and Big Pharma took a page from the cigarette boys,
Sales reps, vacations promoted opioids with much fanfare & noise.

Doctors bought in with a thrill,
So many offices became a pill mill.

The flood gates open wide and for too long,
Those responsible said they were not to blame, same old song.

Ever so slowly we started to reign them in,
And from that vacuum in came heroin.

Cheaper and easier it was to buy,
And oh let's not forget that magnificent high.

Sadly, that's not the worst of it all,
The dealers have upped their game and introduced fentanyl.

It's one of the most addictive drugs out there for me or you, Russian roulette, what's inside you haven't a clue.

So many innocents are dying every day,
Please don't start, is what I say.

Father of Nicholas Jordan Di Marco

LOSS

Pain, loss, suffering, and grief;
Where are the magic words for relief?

We could sit in a corner, rocking sucking our thumb, Would that make
the truth come undone?

The immense pain of your leaving,
Proves how strong our love for you was in our grieving.

We can't and won't tuck your memories away,
But we shouldn't use you to keep others at bay.

We walk a fine line between sanity and despair,
Knowing the truth that you will no longer be there.

So we stumble, fall, and get back on our feet,
We care too much to admit defeat.

Father of Nicholas Jordan Di Marco

THE GENETICS OF DRUG AND ALCOHOL ADDICTION

The Role of Family History

Addiction is due 50 percent to genetic predisposition and 50 percent to poor coping skills. This has been confirmed by numerous studies. One study looked at 861 identical twin pairs and 653 fraternal (nonidentical) twin pairs. When one identical twin was addicted to alcohol, the other twin had a high probability of being addicted. But when one nonidentical twin was addicted to alcohol, the other twin did not necessarily have an addiction. Based on the differences between the identical and nonidentical twins, the study showed 50–60 percent of addiction is due to genetic factors. (1) Those numbers have been confirmed by other studies. (2) The other 50 percent is due to poor coping skills, such as dealing with stress or uncomfortable emotions.

Nick's Backyard Memorial

A thousand words won't bring you back. I know because I've tried. Neither will a thousand tears; I know because I've cried.

Nick, his sister and his dad.

Nick's friends paying tribute
Nick's backyard memorial

Me (Fred G. Di Marco) at a Narcan training class

Why do some people become addicted while others don't? Family studies that include identical twins, fraternal twins, adoptees, and siblings suggest that as much as half of a person's risk of becoming addicted to nicotine, alcohol, or other drugs depends on his or her genetic makeup. Pinning down the biological basis for this risk is an important avenue of research for scientists trying to solve the problem of drug addiction.

ENABLING ADDICTION

ARE YOU LOVING SOMEONE TO DEATH?

YOU ENABLE THEM BY:

Giving Money When Asked
They will beg, plead, and threaten. They will say they are starving, need medical attention, or need gas. Be aware – they are using that money to support their habit.

Paying For A Car
A car, insurance, or gas – while needed for work or school, she is also using it to meet her supplier, or transport drugs to other people.

Paying For A Phone
You want to stay in contact, now that he is gone for days at a time. His cell phone contains the numbers to dealers. Providing the phone helps him get high.

Paying For Or Providing A Place To Live
Providing her with money for rent, utilities, a hotel room, or room at your home gives her a place to use. He will bring drugs into your home, and get high there every day. One day, he is lifeless in your home.

Bailing Them Out Of Jail
Bailing her out of jail and bringing her home only enables her to continue the behavior. Help her by not bailing her out.

YOU LOVE THEM BY:

Giving Them Food
Meet your son at a restaurant and buy him a meal. It provides you the opportunity to stay connected and ask if he's had enough of his addiction.

Seeking Professional Help
Contact an interventionist. A professional intervention dramatically increases your chances of getting your loved one into treatment.

Getting Treatment
She needs it. If she had cancer, you would do anything to get it into remission. Treatment is what puts addiction into remission. Paying for rehab is just like providing meds. And far better than paying for a funeral.

Answering The Phone
Stay strong, tell him how much you love and miss him, and always say, "Are you ready to go to treatment?" If he isn't now, he will be.

Treating Addiction Like The Disease It Is
Hoping they will just "stop" it – means that person often stays sick much longer than necessary and the family continues enabling. Arming yourself with the signs and symptoms of addiction significantly increases your chances of getting your loved one into a great treatment program that will treat this disease for life.

A SINGLE STONE

A single stone cast into the water has a ripple effect,
Many waves are caused by the rock you eject.

The addict that you hear about whose life has expired,
think about who's been affected before her memory becomes retired.

The grieving parents of their beloved son,
Truly know that it doesn't affect only one.

Sister or brother coming home from school at the end of the day,
After losing their sibling, what is there to say?

Maybe they were a husband and/or wife,
The one that is left behind, ha not much of a life.

Besides our eyes and ears we must open our hearts,
For they are people, just like us and deserve a new start.

Father of Nicholas Jordan Di Marco

A NORMAL DAY

Sandy woke up like pretty much every other day, her knee hurting like hell.
Reached for a little bottle of Oxy's and started her morning routine.
Oh well.

Tyler after a shower looked in the mirror, didn't like what he saw.
A few inhales later he was wrapped in a warm embrace of numbness and awe.

Amanda was on a mission, a deadline to meet, a proposal to complete.
Finished and done, time for some fun. She was never going to admit defeat.

Logan, couldn't really tell you how it all began, now sleeping under the moon.
Trying to make it through the day, desperately hanging on to his needle and spoon.

Four completely different lives with a lethal common thread.
Without our help there is a good chance they could all end up dead.

Father of Nicholas Jordan Di Marco

AN EVIL ROMANCE

When we first met it was not love at first sight,
Addiction to you was something I thought I could fight.

Your love was like nothing I ever felt before,
Oh, I wish I never had opened that dark door.

You were created in the depths of hell,
Once tasted I was bound by your spell.

I will always remember our first embrace,
Never to be imitated, just a dream to chase.

Of your bonds I truly wish to break free,
Shackled by self-loathing and misery.

There are some who would from your grasp release me,
While others believe this is just where I should be.

This vile relationship must come to an end,
Your hold on me I must break and end.

Father of Nicholas Jordan Di Marco

SEVERAL PEOPLE WALK PAST AN ADDICT ON THE STREET AT DIFFERENT TIMES

The first is disgusted by their appearance and quite openly shows their disdain.

The second looks over with a smirk and a sneer, gives a very sarcastic remark about having a good day and moves on.

The third stops, offers some food, clothing and shelter and then continues on their way.

Of these four people, who was the father/mother, first responder, neighbor and/or government official?

Answer: all of them!

Father of Nicholas Jordan Di Marco

COMMON RELAPSE TRIGGERS AND HOW TO MANAGE THEM

Relapse triggers can be broken into a few groups: emotional, mental, environmental, and those that are easily overlooked. Here we have listed the ten most common relapse triggers and what to do to avoid them.

1. HALT: Hungry, Angry, Lonely, and Tired

The acronym HALT is used to describe high-risk situations for those in recovery. When you are aware of this, you can be vigilant in preventing yourself from entering those states.

If recovery is your priority, then making sure you avoid becoming too hungry, angry, lonely, or tired will also need to become priorities. This may mean planning meals, sticking to a strict sleep schedule, and attending support groups.

2. Emotions

Perceived negative emotions often lead people to use drugs or alcohol in the first place and can easily lead a person back to their drug of choice.

It is, however, impossible to avoid feeling sad, angry, guilty, or lonely all the time. Experiencing these emotions is normal and an important aspect of recovery (and life)—but they are uncomfortable! Learning how to cope with your emotions as they arise without the use of drugs and alcohol will be essential in early recovery.

3.   Stress

Stress could possibly be the number one addiction relapse trigger because of its broad range of effects on the mind and body. HALT can lead to stress, as can a thousand other circumstances that will differ for each individual. Losing a job or loved one, increased responsibility at home or work, and health problems can all create increased stress. The key here is being proactive about stress prevention and being mindful (and honest) about what causes stress for you.

4.   Overconfidence

Becoming overconfident in recovery puts you at risk for relapse. Having self-confidence is necessary, but becoming overconfident to the point of complacency crosses a line from healthy confidence to overconfidence and relapse risk.

After some time in recovery, as life starts to even out, you may begin to feel like you no longer need to follow your relapse prevention plan. You might think you are strong in your recovery and put yourself in increasingly risky situations—while also no longer working a recovery program. This is a definite recipe for disaster.

Stay humble by giving back to others if you can, and always remind yourself that addiction is a chronic disease; no matter how strong you feel you will never be able to have "just one."

5.   Mental or physical illness

Depression, anxiety, and other underlying mental illnesses can trigger drug or alcohol relapse. Physical illness and pain can also put you at risk for relapsing, as your body is stressed.

Prescription drugs for mental and physical illnesses can be mind-altering and trigger addiction and addiction relapse. Sharing that you are in recovery with your doctor and being insistent about providing nonaddictive prescription drug alternatives is important.

Get treatment for any underlying mental illness and monitor your thinking and feeling with a journal to help notice when you are slipping into old patterns.

6. Social isolation

Reluctance to reach out to others or form a sober support system through AA or another recovery group can lead to social isolation and loneliness. The more you become socially isolated, the easier it is to rationalize drug or alcohol use to yourself.

Social anxiety can also be a struggle for many recovering addicts, which is why having a counsellor or sponsor can help you avoid social isolation. Make forming a sober support network a priority in your recovery.

7. Sex and relationships

A common, but often ignored suggestion is to avoid dating in recovery for the first year. There are many reasons for this, one being that new romantic relationships can put you at risk for relapse. A breakup with your new partner could lead you back to using due to emotional stress. A potential cross over from your initial addiction to a sex or love addiction; or using relationships to fill the void left by sobriety also create increased risk for relapse.

Remind yourself why it is important to avoid relationships in early recovery, and if you have more than a year of sobriety under your belt follow these tips for dating in recovery to help make sure your transition to the dating world does not sabotage your sobriety.

8. Getting a promotion or new job

Positive life events are often overlooked as relapse triggers. Getting a promotion or new job can lead to an urge to celebrate. You may fall into the false idea that is celebrating with a drink or drug "just this once" will be okay. Increased income can also trigger thoughts of being able to afford your drug of choice.

While a promotion or other positive event is exciting and can boost your confidence, it may also come with added responsibility, pressure, and stress. That's why it is important to make a plan for how you will celebrate without drugs or alcohol in advance of actually being in this situation.

9.   Reminiscing about or glamorizing past drug use

Relapse is a process. If you find yourself reminiscing about times when you used to drink or use in a way that overlooks the pain and suffering your addiction caused, this is a major red flag.

Reminiscing can lead to your addictive brain taking over once again. Talking about past use can lead to thinking about future use, and quickly turn into action.

If you find yourself in this pattern of reminiscing, do not ignore it! Talk to a sponsor, counselor, or supportive friend about it—they will help remind you why you chose a life in recovery.

10.   Social situations or places where drugs are available

Another one of the most common relapse triggers is putting yourself in situations where drugs and alcohol are available. It is not always so straightforward, though—simply driving through an old neighborhood or catching the smell of a pub as you walk by can be enough to trigger intense urges to use.

One of the first relapse preventions plans you make should be a list of people, places, and things that are strong triggers for you personally. When doing this, think outside the obvious and ask your sponsor or counselor for help so you're not later caught off guard by an emotion, sight, or smell.

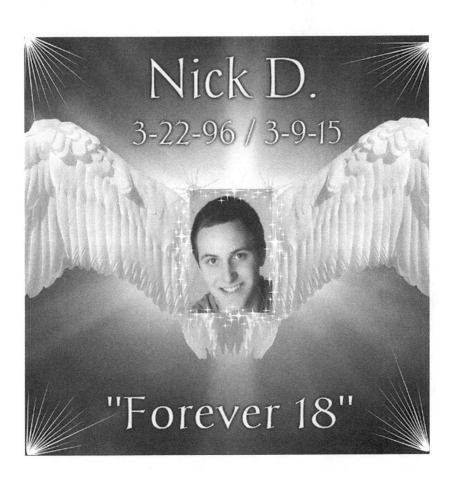

ANGRY

I am angry as hell,
You took my child and left me with dark thoughts on which to dwell.

Stigma and ignorance kept my actions at bay,
Lacking the proper knowledge & resources what was I to say.

Whether mental illness or predisposition, the deck was stacked in your favor,
That complete surrender you did savor.

You cared not if it be husband or wife,
Too many innocents from you have lost a life.

We are now learning more of what and who you truly are,
Your over prescription of opioids has gone too far.

My goal is to live long enough to see the day,
When your evil grip no longer holds any at bay!

Father of Nicholas Jordan Di Marco

EENY, MEENY, MINY, MOE

Catch a user by the arm,
If they resist, my addiction will cause them harm.

Whose life do I wish to destroy today?
The family man on his way to work, trying to earn his pay?

How about the high school football star with the tore-up
Knee, a couple of months on his scripts, it will be so easy.

I like the 4.0 kid who just got her wisdom teeth out,
Here a Perc, there a Perc, she'll be mine without a doubt.

The teens that suffer anxiety and depression are always a plus, they're
the ones that never seem to get put on the right bus.

Let's not forget to add in the casual celebrity,
That's one that I always like to see.

Here's what you folks fail to understand about me,
I don't care who you are, I look for every opportunity!

Black, White, rich or poor even old or young,
No one is spared, once on my path you will come undone.

Father of Nicholas Jordan Di Marco

I DIDN'T KNOW

Who knew addiction was a disease, did you,
I just thought they did what they wanted to.

How about mental health and drug addiction being so intertwined,
We need much more study and research, more information we must find.

The addict is not the person they were meant or wanted to be,
Struggling against the desire constantly.

Families and friends want to help them,
But sometimes stigma and ignorance keep them walled in.

The things that you like to say and do,
How your brain responds by making you feel so good too.

Well opioids do that but oh so much more I am told,
50 times more, your pleasure receptors go into overload!

When you go without and you're going into withdrawal,
Who ever thought a pain like this existed at all?

The stuff you bought from your local dope boy the day before,
Will never be the same, that you can be sure.

The thing I really didn't know,
Is why did you have to go?

Father of Nicholas Jordan Di Marco

ONE, TWO, OR THREE—WHICH SHALL IT BE

Three doors from which you can choose,
Two if picked, you will surely lose.

One door will send you to jail,
Your addiction the system was not meant to treat, in treating you they will fail.

The second door, if you continue to use you will most likely draw your last breath,
Nothing good will come of this and will most probably cause your death.

Now the hardest and most difficult of the three,
Is to go through the door of recovery.

These choices you have been given,
Make the right one and keep on living.

Father of Nicholas Jordan Di Marco

IN VEIN

Looking for my dope boy, standing out in the rain,
How long do I have to wait, feels like I got hit by a train.

Woke up this morning, withdrawals hitting me hard,
Got to get to Walmart return some stolen items for a gift card.

Maybe sneak over to Mom and Dad's while they're out tonight,
Damn, house is locked up good and tight.

All these wrong things you think you need to do,
Because of what the addiction has done to you.

In your heart you want to do what is right,
The disease is telling you not to fight.

This road trip was never meant to end up this way,
Feel trapped inside your own body, no matter what you do or say.

There is a way to break free of your chains,
In the beginning you think you'll go insane.

The time and effort spent will seem most colossal,
I've seen it, Recovery Is Possible!

Father of Nicholas Jordan Di Marco

IT AIN'T EASY BEING ME

I have fallen down the addiction well,
Since then my life has been a living hell.

Struggling every day, always worse than the day before,
What does my future hold, will I be dead on the bathroom floor?

Choice or disease that argument is older than what came first the
chicken or the egg,
How are we going to stop all these deaths, is the question I must beg?

Sadly, the ones that best understand me,
Are the members of my addiction family.

This is not who I am or who I wish to be,
And getting clean is not as easy as 1, 2, 3.

Many obstacles to recovery block our path,
Stigma, ignorance, finances, transportation just do the math.

In its simplest form, three choices they say have I,
Incarceration, recovery or I will most surely die.

Two out of those three are not for me,
I want to be the one in successful recovery!

Father of Nicholas Jordan Di Marco

JUST ONE MORE TIME

I don't want to do this anymore,
I want to be done, not like it was before.

This addiction has sucked me down the drain,
You can't believe the control it has over my brain.

Looking back before I started life wasn't so bad,
True, I didn't understand what I really had.

I'm standing in a crowd yet still completely alone,
Standing next to a fire but chilled to the bone.

Family and friends want little to do with me,
Who I once was is gone, the addiction is all they see.

I want to get better, that much is true,
It's so hard and I don't have much of a clue.

You know what, I'll do it tomorrow just you see,
I won't let this disease get the best of me.

Just one more time, tonight,
Got that right, dead right!

Father of Nicholas Jordan Di Marco

LIFE IN THE IGNORANT LANE

Honey, did you hear about John's wife?
Stage four breast cancer, there goes their life!

Let's plan on going over tomorrow,
See what we can do, help them with their sorrow.

Yesterday Tommy got hurt at work, he will be out for a while,
Me and the boys will stop by, on his face try to put a smile.

Last night at the bar found out Joey's kid got busted for drugs,
I knew something was wrong, those kids are a bunch of thugs.

I don't want our son hanging out with them no more,
Next thing you know, they'll be wanting drugs, trying to score.

You know if they would just raise their kids the right way,
Oh, Savannah's prescription of Xanax got filled today.

If they would teach their kids to make the right decision,
It's a choice not an addiction.

Until we educate the people who hold these ideals to be true,
Countless innocent lives will be lost because they don't have a clue.

Father of Nicholas Jordan Di Marco

MY CONSCIENCE IS SCOTT FREE

It's all their fault, I know this to be true,
No way is it a disease, don't let them fool you.

They made a choice, it wasn't because they were sick,
This is all smoke and mirrors, one slick trick.

Okay, so a couple of doctors gave out a few extra pills,
The addicts kept taking them, getting their thrills.

Yes a few got hooked from a surgery or two,
But it's not like cancer, you don't have a clue.

There might even be some who have a mental condition,
Using as a way of self-medication.

The answer is easy, just say no to whatever they say,
Let them figure it out, tough love all the way.

Well no I don't really know anyone personally who is using you see,
But I'm sure they can quit and stop using, be just like me.

My education and training you ask where it came from,
It's just common sense, do you think I'm dumb?

Father of Nicholas Jordan Di Marco

MY TURN

Look at all those illegals crossing the border,
Send them all back, let's have some law and order.

What's this crap about gay and lesbian pride?
No way, I don't need them by my side.

All these inner-city folks on welfare,
They don't want to work, don't even care.

Drug addicts, why even waste my voice,
We all know it's nothing but a choice.

We don't want them here, send them all away,
Just a waste of my tax dollars that's all I got to say.

Wait, now they are coming after me,
No it's not fair, don't you understand, and can't you see?

Why won't anyone help me, this is so wrong,
No one helped the others, now they're all gone!

Father of Nicholas Jordan Di Marco

NEVER

Did I think Gina and I would stop being friends?
We swore we were BFFs till the end.

Give up football, stop playing the game,
Man, I love it, that's insane.

To lie and steal from my parents that's just a sin,
With the disease of addiction and temptation I gave in.

So many things I wanted to say and do,
Becoming an addict was not on my list to do.

To stand in a crowd yet feel completely alone,
It's a sad feeling, down to the bone.

My father can't or won't understand me,
While my mother hovers and smothers but refuses to see.

Would I have thought that I couldn't just quit,
My brain keeps telling me, just one more hit.

Never do I want to be this way again,
I want successful recovery free from addiction.

Father of Nicholas Jordan Di Marco

OPIOID POKER

The ante is stigma, the lack of sight is ignorance,
Ready for a little game of chance?

I'll call your stigma and raise you a 90-day Oxy prescription,
If you think you got a shot stay in and let's have some fun.

Call, the last hand you took all my Big Pharma,
Shouldn't gloat like that, its bad karma.

Give me two, that should be good enough,
To take that stack of mental disorder stuff.

Just one for me and if I hit,
It will be like the stuff I sell, some really good shit.

I got a hand that can't be beat,
This will leave them dead on the street.

No way can you win, I'm betting it all,
All in even my fentanyl.

The dealer takes a gamble on if he will get caught,
While the risk for the user is "is it death he has bought!"

Father of Nicholas Jordan Di Marco

OPIOID ROULETTE

Give it a shot, take a pill,
Doesn't matter if it was prescribed or you just wanted a thrill.

Once the chamber is loaded,
The life you lived or looked forward to exploded.

Every time you continue to use,
It's a little more of your life that you start to lose.

The excitement, the thrill and or the rush,
Are all gone now, just inside your head is a great big hush.

It's a game that's stacked in the dealer's favor,
All can be lost, and gone your hard-earned labor.

Every time you use it's a throw of the dice,
This type of gamble is a horrible vice.

The risk is not worth the reward,
This is not the future that you looked toward.

Father of Nicholas Jordan Di Marco

CONSERVATORY *of* MUSI

"We Do Recover"

A Concert to Benefit
Safe Passages
*Police Assisted
Recovery Program*

Dedicated to the Memory of
Rob Brandt
Madeline Coy
Nick DiMarco
Tiffany Lovejoy
Dawn Von

Sunday, January 29, 2017
3:00 p.m.

Fanny Nast Gamble Auditorium
Kulas Musical Arts Building
96 Front Street
Berea, Ohio

OUT OF SITE

In the alleys they lie,
Or in the bathroom they may die.

Maybe from a large home up on the hill,
It matters not if they fall victim to the opioid pill.

Raised by God-fearing parents who lived by the good book,
Still ensnared by the disease whose world was shook.

It's of no difference who they were or where they came from,
Once trapped by the addiction your life starts to become undone.

Strangers pass you by with their ideals in their head,
Lacking the knowledge and understanding and sadly don't care if you
become dead. A tragedy in its most deadly form,
so much overdose in the media, has it become the norm?

The how and the why are answers that we need to seek,
If the disease of addiction we wish to defeat.

The innocents that are currently suffering from this horrible calamity,
Need to be given as much support and assistance from the likes of you
and me.

So, on this day of Thanksgiving,
Let's thank God and help those still living!

Father of Nicholas Jordan Di Marco

EFFECTS OF HEROIN

Why?

Why is this happening?

Why me?

Why my kid?

Why do they keep going back to heroin?

Why do they keep choosing drugs over their families?

Coming to terms with the *why* might be essential to your own ability to cope, and more importantly, to be able to understand why "detaching with love" is the only way you can help them.

What happens physically inside the brain when someone uses heroin

There is a tiny area of nerve cells in the frontal cortex of our brains called the "Nucleus Accumbens," otherwise known as the "Reward Center" or the "Pleasure Center."

As heroin enters the blood stream, it makes a beeline directly to that area of the brain, attaches itself to the nerve endings which then causes dopamine to immediately flood the "Nucleus Accumbens" (a.k.a. the pleasure center), creating an unexplainable euphoria of pleasure.

High.

As heroin use continues, the reward center of the brain quickly begins to change. The surges in dopamine, caused by the heroin, teaches the brain to produce less of its own dopamine.

In other words—the more "heroin induced" dopamine surges, the more the brain waits for the heroin to allow the dopamine to release.

The continued heroin induced flooding of dopamine actually causes the brain to lessen its own dopamine receptors in attempts to regulate the surges. Which then requires the user to take in more heroin to get the same "high" as before.

As the nerve endings become lazy—or dependent—to the heroin in order to release dopamine, they also begin to require larger amounts of the heroin to produce equivalent surges.

a.k.a. tolerance

This is where the user starts to be affected in other areas of their lives…

When the pleasure center of the brain (the reward center) has fewer dopamine receptors, and the brains ability to produce and release its own dopamine naturally had lessened…

Other things start to happen.

Things that used to cause natural surges in dopamine in the reward center (or make them happy)—don't anymore

Physically their brains can't be naturally happy.

Things like their favorite meal. Getting compliments. Hanging out and laughing with their friends. Connections with family members. Getting a paycheck after along week of work. Spending time with their kids.

Engaging in these activities normally would cause the brain to naturally release dopamine into the reward center. But after just a short time of using heroin the dopamine receptors have lessened and now require even more dopamine to "make them happy," at the same time the brain is producing less of its own dopamine (or happiness) because it has become dependent on the heroin induced surges of dopamine.

Their brains *literally* requires drugs—heroin (opiates)—to be happy.

The good news is this damage isn't permanent! The brain is an amazing thing! The longer someone goes without using drugs—heroin (opiates)—the more time the brain has to begin to heal and repair the damage done to its receptors and nerves. This healing process can take anywhere from six months (minimal use) to three years (heavy use).

Coming to terms with the science behind addiction and accepting the fact that addiction is *not* a moral shortcoming isn't something you can just decide to "believe" or not.

Although the initial moment when someone decides to use drugs *is* a choice, continued drug abuse is *not*.

Addiction is a disease.

It is not a choice.

It is not an opinion.

It is science.

It is a fact.

It is literally a disease of the brain.

Recovering from addiction is *not* easy. And there is no miracle antidote that will work for everyone.

But recovery is 100 percent possible.

No one is ever truly a "lost cause."

No one.

Ever.

Never lose hope Mommas.

SWEET EMPTY PROMISES

Come unto me for I will make your pain go away,
Let me wrap you in my warm embrace and in the numbness you will
stay.

For the first time when you taste of me so sweet,
It will of an amazing sensation, truly it can't be beat.

I will make you promises of such sweet pleasure,
A feeling like no other, beyond your wildest measure.

And then that which you most fear,
Loss, of job, family, friends, and everything you hold most dear.

For now, you will be my puppet bound by strings,
Through which I will make you do such horrible things.

You will not willingly do these acts and to stop you will try,
My grip is so strong, you will resist, cry and may even want to die.

For today you are stuck in this cursed reality,
Tomorrow cab be your escape to successful recovery.

Have hope, there are many people and groups all around town,
Who wish nothing but the best for you and to keep you above ground.

Father of Nicholas Jordan Di Marco

WHAT DO YOU CALL

A child loses his parent(s), they are called an *orphan*.

A spouse loses his or her partner, they are called a *widow/widower*.

A parent loses their child, they are called?

Vilomah:

Vilomah means "against a natural order." As in, the gray-haired should not bury those with black hair. As in our children should not precede us in death. If they do, we are vilomahed. It comes from an ancient language called Sanskrit.

Fred G. DiMarco with Skylar Williams (successful recovery)!

WHY WOULD DRUG DEALERS LACE HEROIN WITH FENTANYL?

A recent news report gave the reasons why drug dealers now cut heroin with fentanyl. First, fentanyl is relatively cheaper than heroin. In addition, "It is lighter and easier to smuggle," reports Sarah Mars, a researcher on substance abuse at the University of California, San Francisco.

In order to maximize their profits, street-level dealers often mix heroin (which is in short supply) with cheap fentanyl, selling these to unsuspecting users. Although many drug addicts are aware of the dangers of a fentanyl overdose, they cannot tell ahead of time if their supply is laced with fentanyl.

A second major reason why dealers lace heroin with fentanyl is that it takes only a little dose of this hybrid to produce a powerful euphoric high. This is particularly risky as abusers may not be aware that they are taking increasingly *dangerous levels of opioids* than their bodies are used to. Dealers who sell such lethal combination of heroin are reputed to attract more customers, who cannot get "high enough" on regular heroin sold in the streets.

ABOUT THE AUTHOR

Fred G. Di Marco was drafted into the opioid war on March 9, 2015, when his son Nicholas Jordan Di Marco was found unresponsive in their home on the bathroom floor by his twin brother, Adam. His untimely death was due to a mixture of heroin laced with fentanyl. Since that time, Fred has spoken at numerous heroin rallies, high schools, Cuyahoga County Juvenile Drug Court, and the Cleveland Clinic. He's been on panels with the DEA, DOJ, and has critiqued works for the local FBI as well. Working with friends of his son who also suffered from the disease of addiction and/or parents who have lost a child as well, who are in the most unwanted club with Fred. Most recently, his path has taken to putting his feelings on paper and writing poems dealing with this current epidemic. Published in the local newspaper the *Cleveland Plain Dealer* multiple times, *Recovery Today* magazine, *Magnum European* internet magazine as well, and shared multiple times over social media (i.e., Facebook, Twitter, etc.). Fred continues to educate himself as well as the public in hopes of removing the stigma of drug addiction and enlightening the government and public about the chronic brain disease of drug addiction.